Rescue

Elizabeth Nonweiler

first-aid box

stretcher

life jacket

disaster dog

tub boat

seaplane

surf rescue

life raft

breathing apparatus

underground rescue

mountain rescue

air-sea rescue
helicopter

Interesting facts about the pictures

page 2: A **first-aid box** has a collection of things for helping people quickly if they have had an accident or are suddenly ill. It has bandages, antiseptic wipes, tweezers, pills and lots more.

page 3: A **stretcher** is a bed for carrying injured people safely when they have been rescued. Old stretchers had a sheet of material between two poles. New stretchers have legs and wheels.

page 4: A **life jacket** does not sink in water and is brightly coloured. If this girl falls in the sea it will keep her afloat and easy to spot until she is rescued. Old life jackets were made of cork.

page 5: Dogs can smell better than humans, so a **disaster dog** finds people by sniffing the air. This dog is searching for people to rescue after an earthquake caused buildings to fall down.

page 6: When Bangkok, a big city in Thailand, was flooded there were not enough boats to rescue everyone. This man is sitting in a **tub** that is being used as a boat to rescue him from his flooded home.

page 7: **Seaplanes** can take off and land on water. They are good for spotting people in the sea and rescuing them. They can rescue people who are hurt on islands, by landing in a calm bay.

14

page 8: Riding on surf in the sea is fun, but sometimes surfers get hurt or go where it is not safe and cannot get back to shore. **Surf rescue** people watch to see if they need to rescue anyone.

page 9: A **life raft** can be packed away on a ship and blown up if the ship begins to sink. It does not have an engine, but it may have oars for rowing and flares (lights) to help rescuers find it.

page 10: Firefighters wear **breathing apparatus** which gives them clean air to breathe when they rescue people from fires. Smoke has poisonous gases. Too much smoke might kill the firefighters if they breathed it in.

page 11: This team is using ropes to rescue someone who is hurt or trapped in an **underground** cave. They have special equipment to hold the ropes and bring the victim out safely.

page 12: **Mountain rescues** are difficult because there are no roads or flat places to land a helicopter. Instead, helicopters can lower a rope with a harness to carry people to safety.

page 13: This Irish **air-sea rescue helicopter** was searching for people who went missing near the cliffs. A crew member could be lowered on a rope to help lift people into the helicopter.

Letter-sound correspondences

Level 2 books cover the following letter-sound correspondences.
Letter-sound correspondences highlighted in green can be found in this book.

<u>a</u>nt	<u>b</u>ig	<u>c</u>at	<u>d</u>og	<u>e</u>gg	<u>f</u>ish	<u>g</u>et	<u>h</u>ot	<u>i</u>t
<u>j</u>et	<u>k</u>ey	<u>l</u>et	<u>m</u>an	<u>n</u>ut	o<u>ff</u>	<u>p</u>an	<u>qu</u>een	<u>r</u>un
<u>s</u>un	<u>t</u>ap	<u>u</u>p	<u>v</u>an	<u>w</u>et	bo<u>x</u>	<u>y</u>es	<u>z</u>oo	
du<u>ck</u>	fi<u>sh</u>	<u>ch</u>ips	si<u>ng</u>	<u>th</u>in <u>th</u>is	k<u>ee</u>p	l<u>oo</u>k m<u>oo</u>n	<u>ar</u>t	c<u>or</u>n

s<u>ay</u>	b<u>oy</u>	r<u>ai</u>n	<u>oi</u>l	b<u>oa</u>t	<u>ea</u>t	p<u>ie</u>	h<u>igh</u>
m<u>a</u>k<u>e</u>	th<u>e</u>s<u>e</u>	l<u>i</u>k<u>e</u>	n<u>o</u>t<u>e</u>	fl<u>u</u>t<u>e</u> t<u>u</u>b<u>e</u>	<u>ou</u>t	s<u>aw</u>	<u>au</u>thor
h<u>er</u>	b<u>ir</u>d	t<u>ur</u>n	<u>air</u>port	fl<u>ew</u> st<u>ew</u>	bl<u>ue</u> c<u>ue</u>	<u>ph</u>one	<u>wh</u>en